MW01245559

Expert Secrets – Empath

The Ultimate Survival Guide for Controlling Your Emotions, Empathy, Fear, Healing After Narcissistic Abuse, Overcoming Anxiety, and Setting Boundaries From People

Terry Lindberg

Table of Contents

Hey, it's Terry Lindberg,

Before we start, I want to tell you about an exclusive offer just for readers of this book...

When starting your self-help journey, the one thing that you must have in check is your mindset. If your mindset is not up to scratch you are setting yourself up for failure before you have even started.

To have the mindset shift that you'll need to set you up for success; you have to do endless amounts of research to get mental clarity, acquire new daily habits, and much more.

Sounds like hard work, right?

Well yes, it would be, but luckily for you, I have partnered up with Intelligence Mastery. Who are giving away their highly rated course that will give you all of the step-by-step process for shifting your mindset into gear seamlessly!

Best thing about this exclusive offer is it 100% FREE, no-strings-attached. Intelligence Mastery usually charge $297 for this exact same course to their customers

All you need to do to claim your FREE the Ultimate Mindset Course; is in your search browsers URL go to – free.intelligencemastery.com

Once you are on the web page, fill out the required information that Intelligence Mastery asks for; this should only take less than 1 minute of your time. Then straight away in your email inbox you will receive the life changing course that has helped 10,000's of people around the world.

Before reading any further, please do this NOW as I may refer back to some of the units in the course throughout this book!

free.intelligencemastery.com

Who Is Terry Lindberg?

Hello, and Thank you for purchasing a copy from the "Expert Secrets – Self Help Series."

For all of you who do not know who I am, my name is Terry Lindberg, an award-winning Psychologist and Author of the Expert Secrets – Self Help Series. I have dedicated 30+ years of my entire life for innovating the field of psychology and self-help to improve mine and 1000's of other's lives across the globe ranging from top CEO's in their area to the best athletes, and even just regular individuals.

The one thing I can say about everyone who I have worked with is that they see dramatic changes in their lives following my teachings. My teachings help them to push through barriers they never thought they could get through. In most cases, the same outcome happens; they witness a switch go off in their mind, showing them the human brain is far more powerful than they could ever think was imaginable.

Throughout the entire 30+ years of my life studying in the field of psychology and self-help, I have acquired wisdom and unique experiences from the people who I have worked alongside and interviewed. The vast amount of knowledge that I have gained is everything that I will be passing onto you within this book.

This guide is not like any other self-help book out there, as to be honest 99% of self-help books on the market are not even made by someone within the field. They have partnered up with a ghost-writer to produce the contents of the book, then packaged and marketed to you as if it was made by someone who has experience in that topic.

The information that I will share with you has proof of concept and will actually assist you at whatever point you are on your journey.

Have you ever heard of the theory "The Golden Nugget" when

reading a book? This theory means that an entire book could be irrelevant to the topic, but yet there could be one "Golden Nugget" of information that could be life-changing.

Because of this theory, I want you to be prepared and make sure for the the length of this entire book that I have your full attention. By the way, if you didn't notice that the sentence before said "the" back to back, you're not paying enough attention.

Drop everything you are doing, focus on in, and be prepared to take notes. You may be only one sentence away from changing your life forever.

If you learn or like anything about the content, you have consumed when finished. An honest review is always appreciated for helping me make better content in the future.

Now let's get started...

Introduction

Empaths are extraordinary beings. They are among the kindest, warmest, and most luminous people I have ever known. Being around them can very frequently feel like an explosion of wellbeing and positivity, precisely because these people wear their hearts on a sleeve and share every single bit of their beings with the world around them.

Empaths are excellent teachers, amazing parents, and unforgettable lovers. They are the best friends one could have and the most dedicated professionals ever. They will go the extra mile for what they believe in—and they will do it with a smile on their face, fully believing in the power of their actions.

Unfortunately, empaths are also vulnerable. Because they absorb energies from the people around them, they often find it hard to dissociate *their* vibe from someone else's. As such, they can very easily become entrapped in abuse, anxiety, fear, and negative emotions, unable to set their true selves apart from those around them.

If you too have been caught in such situations, you might be an empath. Of course, I'll offer a more in-depth definition of what an empath is, but we will tackle that in the first chapter of the book at hand.

If you want to learn more about empaths, how they are defined, and maybe even more importantly, how to make sure that you can control the less beneficial aspects of being an empath, this book is for you. We will start small, with basic information about empaths and, as we move more deeper into the book, we will start to explore the more high-level topics connected to being an empath. By the end of this book, you will know how to protect yourself or someone close who is an empath and make the most out of your psychological typology.

Why would you trust me with something as important as this? I have dedicated more than three decades of my entire life to investigating the field of psychology and self-help. This has helped improve not only my life, but the lives of thousands of other people across the globe. From CEOs to athletes and regular individuals, I have helped a wide range of people from a vast array of backgrounds make the most out of who they are and achieve their *best version of themselves*.

My purpose with this book is to show people that a little bit of training can help them win over the negative parts of being an empath and improve their lives.

Changing the way you perceive yourself as an empath is an essential step to achieving true success in life, precisely because it will allow you to set healthy boundaries and set yourself free from the tyranny of constantly absorbing other people's negativity. Being an empath is amazing, and it can definitely benefit you as long as you know how to control the "adverse effects" of *feeling* what everyone else feels.

I have worked with empaths all my life and let me tell you this: I truly believe they are among the most amazing people I have ever met. Yet empaths are also susceptible to being taken advantage of (consciously or unconsciously), they are susceptible to depression and anxiety, and, at a certain level, they are susceptible to never following their own path (precisely because they are so immersed in what everyone else is experiencing).

Over time, I have learned exactly how to help my patients "reprogram" these tendencies. People have thanked me and have paid me hundreds of times the price of this book to learn the exact same teachings and techniques I will be sharing with you throughout the following pages.

I will teach you how to handle your own empathy in a way that benefits you and those around you so that you can chase your dreams and be *free* from the shackles of excessive sensitivity. Believe it or not, these strategies are much simpler than what they might appear at first—but I have seen their effectiveness with my own eyes and I believe in them with all my heart.

I cannot promise your life will change overnight after reading this book. What I *can* promise, however, is that, by the end of it, you will be fully equipped with the skills and knowledge you need to be able to improve the way you allow your empathy to interact with the world and with your own dreams.

Ever heard of Andy Warhol's words, "They say time changes things, but you actually have to change them yourself" (Warhol, 2020)? Well, it is resoundingly true. Time does change things—but they are not always good changes. Sometimes, time sends us spiraling down into our own negative behaviors and makes things worse. If you don't take control over these tendencies *now*, you will allow time to play its game on you—and the absolute truth is that you are not guaranteed that it will *end well*.

It's important for you to learn how to be a "functional" empath right now. Every minute you spend allowing others to stomp on you is a minute that brings you closer to your own downfall. Even more, every minute you waste your energy on everyone else (and none of it on yourself) is a minute you have lost on building on your true self and achieving your *best version* of it.

The strategies you are about to learn from this book are a game changer. They are not only easy to understand, but they are proven to yield actual results. Every chapter of this book, every paragraph, and every line have been carefully brought together to help you become who you were meant to be in the first place. Follow the tips of advice I will show you in the next pages and the world is yours.

I'm rooting for you. I really am. I believe a world "ruled" by people who know how to *sense* others is a better world, one that has a lot more chance to be *at peace* from every point of view.

Good luck in your journey! Remember: the power to be who you want to be is in YOUR hands, and this book might just be the catalyst to push everything in a (much) better direction for you!

Chapter 1: What Is an Empath?

Put simply, an empath is a person who displays empathy. By definition, empathy is the ability to sense and even experience the same emotions and experiences as others do. For instance, if your friend has lost their cat and you know they loved it a lot, you will empathize with them by feeling sad and anxious about finding their furry friend.

These are just basic definitions, though. Beyond the surface, empaths are incredibly complex human beings able to truly absorb the energies around them—which makes them absolutely amazing from many points of view. At the same time, all the qualities of an empath can very easily turn against them and cause them a series of problems. We will discuss both sides of the coin throughout the book at hand.

When you tell an empath to walk a mile in someone's shoes, they can actually do it. They not only put on the shoes, but adapt their entire being to that pair of footwear and walk the mile as if they were the original owners. This makes empaths amazing friends, mothers or fathers, workers who are true team players and leaders who are truly there for their people.

It also makes them susceptible to absorbing *too* much of the world around them, which might sound like a great idea, except it can completely annihilate the empath's own personality and personal goals.

You don't have to let go of empathy entirely if you want to live a healthy and balanced life. The key is finding the right way to deal with the negative sides of being an empath while still being your kind and honest self.

Over the course of this book, you will learn how to be a successful empath—one who knows how to use your superpowers and yet doesn't give in to the negative energies bombarding you from the exterior.

So, what is an empath?

An empath is a person who experiences the world as if they were the world itself. Some of the defining traits of an empath include the following:

- You always *feel* what your friends and relatives are going through. Sometimes, you can even *feel* what someone on the TV or on the street is going through.
- You don't like crowded places because they feel overwhelming.
- Spending too much time or being too close or intimate with someone can also feel overwhelming to you.
- You usually have a very good intuition, both when it comes to people and when it comes to places and situations in general.
- You feel at home when you are out in nature.
- For you, the term "I don't care" does not really exist.
- You naturally attract people who want to share their problems with you.
- You tend to be sensitive to sounds, light, or smells.
- You avoid conflict at all costs.
- Sometimes, although people are naturally drawn to you, you feel that you just don't fit in entirely.
- You find it quite difficult to set boundaries or say "no" to someone.
- You prefer solitude most of the time, and not because you are antisocial or even an introvert, but because being around people can feel exhausting.
- You are sometimes experiencing a sensory or emotional overload—what you are feeling simply becomes *too much* for you.
- You tend to see the world through a very unique perspective, precisely because you can connect with people, animals, and places at a deeper level than most people.

Empaths are not the ultimate *good*. They do have their dark side, and most of the time this dark side is connected to how they absorb all the influences around them. On the one hand, if an empath is dominated by a negative influence, they too might display negative behavior. On the other hand, even if they are not actually abused or dominated, empaths can absorb too much of the exterior world. As such, they can become stressed, depressed, anxious, and filled with remorse and negativity.

As I was saying before, all these negative sides can be fine-tuned. Like a musical instrument, the empath can create noise or music, and it all lies in the way they manage to fine-tune their sensitive chords.

In the following chapters, I will show you how to determine if you are an empath (and to what degree) and to learn how to embrace and live with your typology. You can truly do amazing things and you can change the world if you put your mind to it, but before you throw yourself in the next big adventure of your life, trying to volunteer and help those less fortunate, you must first deal with yourself.

As an empath, you might not put a lot of emphasis on *you*, but trust me when I say that it is of the utmost importance for you to learn how to be a little selfish every now and again. How can you help the world if the world overwhelms you with every single occasion it gets?

The biggest challenge of being an empath is learning how and when to put yourself ahead of everyone else. When you know how to connect external emotions with everything else within you, you have the power to truly make the world a better place. Believe me, I've seen it happen.

Chapter 2: Are You an Empath?

Sometimes it can be difficult to determine if you are an empath (or to *what extent* you are an empath). As such, this chapter will help you self-assess and see where on the empathy scale you lie.

I believe this step is extremely important because it will allow you to assess your true self in a realistic way. From here, you can choose which of the techniques presented in this book work for you and which might not be suitable for your specific type of empathy.

The rules are simple: read the following questions, answer them, and then count how many positive answers you have. Based on how many "yes" answers you have, you will learn more about the empathy spectrum and where on it you might find yourself.

Let's go!

1. Has anyone ever told you that you are too sensitive or shy?
2. Do you feel mentally and physically affected by arguments?
3. Do you often feel that you don't quite fit in?
4. Do you feel overwhelmed when you are in a crowd and then feel the need to retreat to replenish your batteries?
5. Do you find yourself overeating when you are stressed out or sad?
6. Do you feel that you are overstimulated when you hear certain noises, when you feel certain odors, or when you are around people who talk a lot?
7. Do you prefer to use your own car when you have to go somewhere so that you can leave as early as you want to?
8. Are you sensitive to chemicals or can't stand itchy clothes?
9. Are you easy to startle?
10. Do caffeine or certain types of medication have a strong effect on you?
11. Do you feel that an intimate relationship can easily suffocate you?
12. Is your pain threshold low?
13. Do you tend to run away from society, rather than run towards it?

14. Do you feel that multitasking is difficult and overwhelming?
15. Do you sometimes feel that you absorb people's moods, emotions, or even their physical symptoms?
16. Do you feel the need to retreat and reboot after spending time with difficult people?
17. Do you find yourself rejuvenated when you are in a natural landscape?
18. Do you prefer small groups (or even one-on-one interactions) over large gatherings?
19. Do you prefer to be in small towns or the countryside, rather than in a large city?
20. Do you easily "read" people and know when they say something but they mean something completely different?
21. Have you ever noticed that your mood changes when someone specific is near or walks in a room?
22. Has anyone ever described you as moody?
23. Do you sometimes feel confused by your own emotions and how quickly you can change from one state to another?
24. Can you influence the moods of the people who surround you (be it in a positive way or in a negative one)?
25. Have you ever found yourself spending a lot of time with someone and then picking up on their behavior or way of talking?
26. Do you like being around water?
27. Do you frequently find yourself as the person your friends and family come to when they have a problem they want to talk about?
28. Do you feel physically or emotionally sick when you watch violent movies or scenes on TV or on the internet?
29. Do you sometimes find yourself forgetting about your own person and only wanting to take care of others?
30. Do you believe animals (and even plants) have consciousness?

If You Scored 1 to 7...

You are at least partially an empath. You might experience some of the side effects of being an empath, but overall, what you experience is mild compared to what an extreme empath would. For instance, you might not be triggered by all the violent scenes in a movie, but you might be triggered if the violence is extreme or if it's geared towards people or animals that are generally considered to be more vulnerable (such as children or puppies, for example).

If You Scored 8 to 13...

You are most likely a moderate empath. This means that you tend to be quite sensitive in general and that sometimes you might even feel sick after discussing with someone who talks a lot or someone who displays a negative vibe. Most of the time, you can quickly recover after such "attacks," though, and normally see to your life and activities. You are not completely against social activities and you definitely love being around people, but sometimes, large groups can feel like "too much" for you.

If You Scored 14 to 19...

You are a strong empath. You really do sense the people around you and sometimes you clearly sense that you absorb their energies—both negative and positive. You love being outdoors and you have a very close connection to animals and plants. Also, you try to stay away from noise, from the city, and from overly talkative or loud people or environments. You generally seek quietness and peace in your life and you are much more likely to be seen cuddled with a book than hanging out with thirty unknown people.

If You Scored Over 20...

You are an extreme empath. You not only absorb energies; you allow yourself to be fully immersed in them. Clearly, this tends to have a negative impact on your body and on your mind, as you frequently feel "lost" among everyone else. You find it hard to focus on your own person and on your personal goals and consistently get lost in helping everyone else (which is not bad at all, but it can be very consuming for you and it can make you develop negative emotions). It is also very likely that you are a vegetarian or a vegan and that you surround yourself with plants and animals as much as you can. You are a kind, open heart, but the same heart can be your biggest enemy too.

Now that you know more about what type of empath you are, you will be able to assess your situation with a little more clarity. As such, you will also be able to choose the best techniques to use in moderating your empathetic tendencies and making the most out of your typology.

Chapter 3: How to Embrace Your Gift

Being an empath might be seen as a weakness by those who don't know better, but it is exactly the opposite. Over the years, I have learned that empaths possess an immense power that makes them almost superhuman: the power to connect with people and to understand their pains and their joys. When you learn how to control this power, the world can be yours. But even more than that, you can reshape the world according to your own vision.

I strongly believe everyone should accept who they are and work on moderating their negative tendencies, instead of suffocating their character and personality (which is actually the worst thing to do regardless of who you are and where on the psychological spectrum you might be).

Empaths are no exception to this. Yes, it can be truly tiresome and nerve-wracking to be constantly in the wind of everyone else's energies, but once you learn to master this sensitivity, you can use it to help people, to help yourself, and to rethink the way in which the world *lives*.

Embracing your empathy is not about letting go and allowing it to "roam wild" through your veins, but about allowing yourself to love, and sense, and connect with people while not allowing yourself to fall into the deep and dark pit of despair when the same people do not answer your concern in return (and even more, might take advantage of your kindness).

How do you get there? How do you truly embrace being an empath, with its goods and its bads, and how do you turn off the constant struggle in your mind between being what "society" expects you to be and being who you truly are?

Here are some tips you might want to keep in mind:

1. Acknowledge who you are. The "WHY" doesn't matter here, but the "WHO" definitely does. You are who you are, and you should not feel like you have to fit into any kind of pattern or mold. The world around you might be individualistic and mean, and some people might want to

put you down for your empathy. That doesn't matter: when you learn to really accept who you are, you learn that you have the power to not only step aside from negative people, but also show them that kindness and compassion are, indeed, the *only* way.

2. Understand that you are not a victim. On the contrary, empaths are among the strongest people who have ever graced this earth. Not only do they have the superpower to sense what's going on even when words don't spell it out, but they actually have the power to spread positivity into the world—because, yes, when you learn how to "control" your empathy, you can use it to share good vibes too, not only to absorb the energies around you.

3. Be proud of who you are. Some might have called you a wallflower or they might have downright told you that you are overly sensitive. You know what, though? You are amazing, and take this from someone who has seen many empaths succeed and conquer their dreams like nobody else can.

4. Accept that you might sometimes have to step away. You might have to step away from situations of vibrations that do you no good. You might have to step away from people who hurt you (intentionally or not). You might even have to step away from social situations to recharge. Do not fight this. Allow yourself to be who you are and move at your own pace. Remember, you are the choreographer behind your dance, so you can set the tone, the rhythm, and the music!

5. Surround yourself with things that heal you and make you feel good. It might be plants or dogs or cats or kind people who want to help others. It might be books or movies or oil paints and canvases. Whatever it is, surround yourself with it and allow it to replenish your positive vibes as much as you can.

6. Surround yourself with people who appreciate you for who you are and who understand that you are sensitive. You might not always be able to run away from people who simply don't "get" you, but you can definitely try to surround yourself with people who are positive, as much as possible. Doing this will help you understand that there's absolutely nothing wrong with you, and that you deserve to love yourself *as you are*.

You really need to celebrate your empathy because out of all people, you are probably the one that is closest to any kind of ideal of goodness and prosperity. You are the kind of person who can move mountains because you have learned from a very early age that there's an inherent strength to you. Every tear you have ever dropped and every ounce of sadness or grief you might have ever felt are now fortifying your being and allowing you to overcome any kind of obstacle that might come your way.

All you need now is to embrace who you are and learn how to use it to your benefit and to the benefit of those you love and appreciate.

Chapter 4: How Empathy Affects Your Daily Life

In times of trouble, we all hear how empathy is absolutely crucial. We heard it around 9/11, and we heard it when the world first started grappling with a highly contagious disease in 2020. We hear it when there's natural catastrophes happening, and we hear it when people we know go through sad, grieving moments of their lives.

Few people think of how truly empathetic souls feel about all this and how drained they can feel at the end of the day when they have absorbed all the bad news, all the tears, and all the fear of the world within themselves.

Unless you are an empath, you really cannot know how it feels to be consistently at the mercy of everything surrounding you and to not be able to control your emotions and your own fears to be able to move along with your life, your dreams, your goals.

To understand why you need to change and adjust some things in your life and why you need to switch your behavior a little and balance it out, you must first understand how empathy affects your daily life.

We all know empathy can have a great effect on people who need compassion, kindness, and forgiveness in their lives. We know empathy can go a very long way when communities are facing tough times. We definitely know a drop of empathy can really make the world a better place from a number of points of view. And many people don't know it, but empathy has been scientifically proven to be good for business too (Ross, 2018).

Still, how does empathy affect an empath's life? How does it change the way they see... *everything*?

Here are some negative side effects of being an empath. For example:

1. Being so empathetic can make one feel divided between two opposing forces. Empaths can feel good and bad at the

same time precisely because they allow themselves to be influenced by everything external and because they cannot find a balance between what comes from within and what comes from the outer world.

2. An empath's deep understanding of relationship mechanics can make them susceptible to being more vulnerable to toxicity. Empaths know very well what others are feeling, and for that reason, they might develop a toxic behavior or they might become the prey of an even more toxic person (such as a narcissistic abuser, for example).

3. Empaths can very easily get tired of being the constant emotional sponge of the world. It is, indeed, more than tiresome to have to live with a "condition" that makes you absorb everything around you: emotions, energies, and even barely enunciated thoughts.

4. Although they are so great with feeling people's moods and emotions, empaths do not always have successful relationships. Many times, this happens because empaths have learned to not let their guards down. Other times, this happens because they are too overwhelming in their love. Empaths have to learn how to "dose" their empathy towards their loved one (and they have to make sure they learn how not to fall victim to an abusive narcissist).

5. Many empaths live in a constant inner struggle, fighting between their tendency to absorb external emotions and their natural needs to allow *themselves* to be in a world where every step outside of the house can feel like an emotional rollercoaster. This conflict can lead to a series of mental health issues, including anxiety, depression, and even personality disorders.

It's hard not to love an empath, but if you are one or if someone you love is one, you must also know about the dark side of such a personality. This way, you will be able to manage it well and you will be able to accept yourself or your loved one with the related ups and downs.

So, how does empathy affect one's life, really?

It can affect you in so many ways it is nearly impossible to explain all of them in just a few lines. On the one hand, it affects your view of the world—on the one side empathizing with it, on the other side so emotionally drained, you want to permanently withdraw from everyone.

Secondly, being an empath affects your personal relationships. Sometimes, when you constantly absorb everything around you, you find it difficult to focus your attention on your loved ones too. Even more, you might carry with you rancor and malice from your previous experiences, and it might be hard not to judge everyone around you through the perspective of your story.

Last, but definitely not least, being an empath can make you feel drained. Constantly tired. Constantly sad. Constantly out of tune with most groups you hang out with. Constantly worn out.

As I mentioned earlier in the book, the good news is that empaths do not have to suffer all these "side effects." They can learn how to calibrate their super ability to empathize and live healthy lives, both from a physical and from a mental point of view.

Hey, it's Terry Lindberg,

As mentioned at the start of this book, you have an exclusive offer available to you for a short period of time.

In case you forgot to claim your 100% FREE, no strings attached ultimate mindset course by Intelligence Mastery.

Please can you make sure to do so NOW!

The reason for this is in the next coming chapters I will be discussing and referring back to parts of the course that Intelligence Mastery has created for you to improve your mindset.

It will be pivotal to have this course available at all times as when learning about self-improvement strategies, the ultimate mindset course will guide you to implement these strategies in a quick and effective manner.

In case you forgot how to claim your FREE copy of the Ultimate Mindset Course, search in your search browsers URL – free.intelligencemastery.com

Remember, before reading any further, please do this NOW as I will refer back to parts of the course throughout this book!

free.intelligencemastery.com

Chapter 5: Living as an Empath

Empaths experience life in ways other people cannot even understand. They'll cry when they see a sad movie as if they were the main character. They will be touched by Coca-Cola commercials around Christmas. They will be genuinely happy for those people on TV who get a makeover and feel renewed and empowered.

That sounds wonderful because, in the end, what is there better about a human being than the power they have to connect with others? But when the empath cannot completely dissociate themselves from others, things can very easily spiral out of control.

Living as an empath can feel like you're always in the battle zone and you don't have much to protect yourself with (or at least not *naturally*). As such, empaths need to build a life for themselves where they are allowed to feel sane and healthy—a life that might not always fit the "normal" paradigm, but that fits the needs of the empath.

For example, empaths might need to:

- Have enough alone time, even when they are in a relationship. Empaths cannot be around people for too long without feeling exhausted, and as such, they need to withdraw and recharge their batteries with regularity. Sometimes, this might mean that they have to withdraw from their life partners as well.

- Feel in touch with nature as much as possible. Most empaths feel at home when they are outdoors, so it's important for them to reconnect with Mother Nature on a regular basis. You might not be able to hike every other week, but even so, walks around the park, surrounding yourself with plants and animals, and maybe even cultivating your own small garden can all help.

- Have meaningful and deep conversations. Empaths frequently feel the need to talk to people, but not just random gibberish. They want their discussions to be meaningful, filled with wisdom and emotion. They want their conversations to be deep. You can do this with your friends, with your partner, or even online in various discussion groups.

- Stay away from energy vampires. This might sound crazy, but some people are real energy vampires. Consciously or not, they "suck" the energy out of those around them – and empaths tend to be more affected by this typology. Try to stay as far away as you can from energy vampires. They can have a massively negative effect on you.

- Find partners who understand their need to withdraw and recharge. As mentioned above, empaths frequently feel the need to withdraw from social situations and this might sometimes include their life partners as well. As such, it is of the utmost importance for you to find a special someone who understands your need for space. Anyone who doesn't will eventually make you feel drained and tired.

- Practice mindfulness. There are multiple ways to do this, and we will discuss them more in the following chapters. What you definitely need to know is that mindfulness *does* have a positive effect on empaths who want to ground themselves and balance out their tendencies.

- Use journaling to relieve themselves from past trauma. Many empaths suffer from past trauma that makes their sensitivity levels even higher at the present moment. Journaling (as well as, of course, *therapy*) can help with this. We will also discuss this in the following chapters, but for now you can keep in mind that you should consider mindfulness techniques to achieve balance between your past and your present.

- Work in an environment that fosters peace of mind and positive vibes. This includes the actual physical environment as well as the moral support and the vibes you get from the people you work with. Obviously, a healthy work environment is important for everyone, but it tends to be even more crucial for empaths, especially since they are prone to absorbing the negativity around them.

- Fill their lives with hobbies and projects. It doesn't matter if it's painting, sewing, or feeding pigeons, little hobbies can help you ground yourself, they can help you achieve balance, and they can help you grow as a human being in the direction you want to grow.

Living as an empath might not seem that much different than living as any other type of person. And yet, it is. As an empath, you are not naturally "armed" with the energy shields you need to function fully in a world filled with emotions. As such, you need to learn how to build up these shields while still allowing emotions to get through every now and again.

Chapter 6: Controlling Your Emotions

One of the hardest parts of being an empath is learning how to keep your emotions in check. Crying at emotional ads and donating money for every charity you see on social media are nice, but everything in excess can be harmful (for everyone, not just empaths). As such, it is of the utmost importance for you to learn how to control your emotions without entirely leaving your high levels of empathy behind.

You need to understand that your emotions make you an absolutely beautiful human being, but that wearing all these sensitivities on your sleeve can hurt you in the long run and can prevent you from achieving your goals. At the same time, you also need to understand that building stone-cold shields around your emotions is not a solution either. Not only are these shields likely to break sooner than you think, but they will inevitably turn you away from your true self as well—and that is not something you want.

So, how do you control your emotions as an empath? These tips of advice will help:

- Always give yourself the time to shake off the accumulated emotions. It's OK to not want to go out with your friends every Friday night. It's OK to just want to stay at home with your cat and a book. It's OK to turn off social media every now and again. Always give yourself time off from people. Everyone needs this, but empaths need it even more than anyone else.

- Learn how to meditate "guerilla-style." This might sound like an oxymoron, but it's a technique I've noticed to be quite effective in managing the emotions of empaths. What this tactic involves is knowing to accept when you are overwhelmed by emotions and simply taking a few minutes of "time off" to meditate. It's important to start the meditation process as soon as possible, so that you don't allow yourself to be decenterd by even more emotions coming from the exterior.

- Learn how to spot when your empath self needs you to take action. For instance, if someone asks you to do something you are not comfortable doing, simply say "no." If your friends are wearing perfume that troubles your senses, learn to politely tell them to refrain from wearing it. If you find yourself overeating to "hide" your emotions, practice guerilla meditation. Learn to distinguish when you are triggered by your empathetic self and strategize how to deal with these triggers in a healthy and balanced way.

- Learn to let go. Not only are empaths troubled by a lot of emotions *in the present*, but they are very frequently troubled by past emotions and trauma as well. It's easy to understand why empaths can very easily crumble under the weight of all these feelings, and it is easy to see why *letting go* becomes even more crucial in their cases than in anyone else's.

- Learn to process your emotions. Managing your sensitivity doesn't mean you have to shove all your feelings deep down and never touch them again. Sooner or later, they will burst out and explode, and that can be a real catastrophe for you. Instead, learn to process emotions by "filing" them in an organized way and talking about them with a therapist, a trusted friend, or a life coach. You should be doing this regularly to make sure the strategy is effective.

- Celebrate the small things. We cannot always be surrounded by massive successes—so massive that they can even block out all the negative vibes absorbed by an empath. As such, it is important for empaths to learn how to celebrate the small victories and fill their lives with the positive vibes this brings with it. A job well done at work and a slice of cake shared with a coworker, buying a new pair of yoga pants to celebrate a fitness milestone, getting a small gift for your significant other for taking care of house chores—these small things can fill your heart with joy and your life with positive vibes. You really need this!

- Practice deep breathing. Whenever you feel overwhelmed by emotion, allow yourself to simply take a break and practice a bit of deep breathing. Ideally, you want to do this from your diaphragm (abdomen) and focus solely on the act of breathing. This will help you find your center of balance and not allow your emotions to take over.

You may never be able to fully control your emotions (and, in fact, that's not what you're after anyway). However, with practice, you can learn how to calibrate all your feelings and reroute them towards purposes and goals that are more positive and bring you closer to achieving your biggest dreams.

It might take time to learn how to manage your emotions in a healthy way, but remember that life is a learning process any way you take it, so enjoy the ride and make the most of it!

Chapter 7: Healing After Narcissistic Abuse as an Empath

As odd as it might sound, empaths are very frequently attracted to narcissistic people, and the reciprocal is valid too, as many narcissists are attracted to empaths. Quite clearly, this type of relationship is doomed from the very beginning because the narcissist will consistently "eat" the energy resources of the empath and the empath will keep on giving and giving until they are reduced to nothingness on the inside.

Narcissistic abuse is not always about physical abuse (although these cases are quite frequent too). More than anything, narcissistic abuse is about emotional and psychological abuse—about dominating the other person through behavior and words. Narcissists will frequently appear as extremely charming, intelligent, and even downright giving at first, making them the perfect match for an empath. In time, however, they will reveal their true colors.

Unfortunately, by the time the empath realizes what is going on (if they ever fully realize it), the cycle of abuse is fully installed and the empath's batteries feel almost entirely dependent on the narcissist's behavior and words.

The narcissist will put the empath down on a regular basis and they will then falsely lift them up as well, creating a never-ending cycle of mystery in which none of the partners are actually happy (not even the narcissist, even though it might sometimes seem that they are doing all of this out of sheer cruelty).

It is not impossible for an empath to leave a narcissistic abusive relationship. It takes becoming fully aware of their partner's true behavior, and it most definitely takes a lot of determination. Sadly, it frequently requires a lot of courage as well, especially when the abuse has escalated to physical abuse patterns.

Healing after a narcissistic abuse relationship can also take a lot of time. Sometimes, years or even decades can go on before the empath will be able to see their trauma with a completely cool approach.

Some of the main things an empath can do to heal after such a relationship include the following:

- Accept that this situation is not good for you and that you truly had to leave that relationship. You might feel drawn back to it, but every time you do, remind yourself of all the bad times and of how negative an influence this relationship was on you.

- Change your negative thinking patterns. Most people who get into abusive relationships end up there because of certain thinking patterns that are ingrained in their minds. Although quite well-rooted, these patterns can be removed and reshaped into positive ones. For instance, mantras like "I am good enough" and "I deserve having a great life" can help you remove all the negative thinking patterns of the abusive relationship.

- Love yourself—and show it. Show yourself love in the way you move and in the way you eat, in the way you allow yourself to go to sleep when you need it and in the way you pamper yourself with a little treat every now and again. More than anything, show yourself love by never going back to your bad relationship (and never getting in one again).

- Don't think of yourself as a victim, and much less a perpetual one. You have been hurt, but this is none of your fault. You have gone through a truly overwhelming situation, but you are now on the other side, ready to take life by its horns and win the game. You are not a victim. You are a survivor.

Of course, there is a lot more we could say about empaths healing after abusive relationships with narcissists. We could write an entire library on *just* this specific topic, but the main points are here in this chapter. The essence lies in knowing how to disconnect yourself from a narcissist, not just physically, but at an emotional and psychological level too.

Chapter 8: Setting Boundaries With People

As I have repeated throughout this book, it is of the utmost importance for an empath to learn how to set healthy boundaries in their dealings with people. To make it clear, *everyone* should know how to set boundaries, not just empaths. It just happens that this typology is more prone to both not knowing how to set boundaries and simply allowing other people's feelings and energies to *invade* them.

Setting boundaries can be tough, in general, and even more so when you are an ultra-sensitive person who wouldn't hurt a fly and wouldn't say "no" even if it were the last thing they did.

How does an empath set healthy boundaries with people? Here are some things you might want to keep in mind:

- First and foremost, understand what a boundary is. Or, said another way, understand that a boundary is not a bubble to lock yourself in and it is not a wall to put between you and people. It is also not a way to run away from responsibilities, it is not a lack of care or compassion, and it is not a way to block out *all* emotions.

- Instead, understand that boundaries are healthy ways to say "no" and dissociate yourself from the energies surrounding you without blocking them or your personal emotions.

- Practice awareness. Meditation and other mindfulness techniques can help you in time, by making you more aware of the present moment. In turn, this will make it easier for you to be aware of what is going on with you and your emotions *when they happen*. The more aware you are, the more likely it is that you will easily find ways to discern between what should be done and what can be set as a boundary.

- Visualize yourself in the moment. When you feel overwhelmed and feel that you should be setting a boundary but aren't sure if it's appropriate, try to analyze your situation for a bit. Think of how you feel and why you feel like that. Also, think of what is stressful or challenging about the current situation.

- Learn to know what is acceptable for you and what is not acceptable for you. Everyone is different here, so the key to knowing when to set boundaries is knowing who you are and what you are OK with. It is your right to set boundaries in whatever situations you feel uncomfortable, but in order to know when your boundaries are working to your advantage, you must first learn what "flies" with you and what doesn't.

- Learn to trust your intuition. As an empath, your superhero-like intuition is one of the most amazing qualities you possess. Trust it. Chances are that your inner voice is advising you well when it comes to setting healthy boundaries from (certain) people.

- Commit yourself to your boundaries. Once you have told someone about your need to set a bit of distance between the two of you, make sure you commit to your promise. Doing otherwise will only worsen your situation (and it might make the other person perceive you negatively as well).

- Learn how to clearly explain your need for boundaries. You don't have to be snappy or impolite in any way. However, you *do* have to be clear, concise, and as diplomatic as possible. A simple "I am not comfortable with this and I would very much like to not take part in it" can go a long way when you say it right.

Boundaries are not a complete dissociation from the world around you. They are a bit of space you leave between you and other people when you feel uncomfortable with certain situations or simply with getting too close to them.

Yes, you can set boundaries with friends and relatives as well, not just with strangers. Given that you are surrounded mostly by people whom you know, it is actually expected from you to healthy boundaries between you and them (as well as between you and their emotions).

Chapter 9: Grounding Techniques to Help You Center Yourself

Stress affects everyone, but it tends to be even more painful for empaths who experience stress coming from a multitude of sources. Aside from money, jobs, and the economy, factors frequently cited among the most common causes of stress by WebMD (2020), empaths frequently have to deal with the stress of handling negative emotions coming from their surroundings, from their partners, from their family, from their coworkers, and, in the worst-case situations, *from the entirety of the world itself.*

Grounding techniques are usually used to help those who suffer from stress, but they are very commonly recommended to empaths precisely because they experience everything in the *superlative*. In fact, of all the tips and techniques presented in this book, grounding tactics are among the most popularly used (and among those that show the best effects as well).

Knowing how to center yourself will help you dissociate yourself from situations and people who fill you with negativity (or whose feelings are just too much for you). Born in the ancient Japanese practice of Aikido, centering is a practice that allows you to recollect yourself, focus, and make non-emotional decisions on the spot (on what to say, how to react, or what to do next, for example).

Here are some tips to help you *ground* yourself:

- Understand what *grounding* refers to. In essence, what Aikido says is that we are all made of energy (called "ki"). When facing stressful situations, this energy disperses chaotically around the body, and the purpose of grounding is to bring all this energy back to your core, from where you can control it and from where you can rethink your position towards a specific situation.

- Find your center. Although this center is not actually physical, many people report actually feeling it around their navel. The core of your body is where your center should be located—the place where your energy is stored and the place from which you can disperse energy throughout the body in a controlled and balanced way.

- Deep breathing. Deeply breathing in (by exercising your diaphragm) can help you ground yourself even in the most adverse situations. A lot of people do this naturally when they feel stressed out (they simply start to breathe in and out in a controlled way). The reason it works is because deep breaths will focus your entire being on a simple action that happens *inside* of you. As such, this action will also help you find your ground and redirect your energy.
- Redirect the flow of energy in your body. Some people imagine the *ki* energy in their body as a flow of light. Others experience it like a current or a buzz. Everyone is different, and you will definitely find your "flow" as well. Once you have found your center, redirect the energy that stresses you out toward it and allow nature and breathing to calm you down.

In addition to the actual grounding techniques, there are also some tips that might help you *ground* in a more efficient way. For instance:

- Eating healthily will fuel your body with good nutrients and it will allow your mind to focus on controlling and managing your emotions, rather than focusing on what is for dinner.
- Water is absolutely crucial as well. Nearly two thirds (USGS, 2020) of our bodies are made out of water, so it makes sense that we should make sure our hydration levels are on point. Get your eight glasses of water every day and allow it to cleanse your body and your energy flow with it.
- Meditation and other mindfulness techniques. Regular meditation sessions, yoga, tai-chi, and even praying are all mindfulness techniques. They focus on allowing yourself to *be* in the moment. Some of them shift your chaotic train

of thoughts to a single one. Others shift it to your breath, movements you have to make, or poses you have to keep. Their main goal is to train your mind to stay in one "place." The more trained your brain is in doing this, the easier it will be for you to ground yourself when the situation requires it.

- Get creative. Painting, singing, sculpting, crafts—they are a unique form of mindfulness in their own right. If you love getting creative, do it regularly. It will enable you to cleanse your thoughts and your emotions, so that you achieve a more balanced self on a day-to-day basis.

Finding your inner center of balance as an empath is just as crucial for you as the physical center of balance is for an acrobat. Take your time in practicing grounding techniques. Nobody nails it the first time, but practice *will* make you better.

Chapter 10: Additional Strategies for Coping

An empath's greatest qualities can become their worst enemies, precisely because they can end up "eating them up" from the inside. If these tendencies are not controlled, empaths can *fall* into the deepest pits of sadness, anxiety, and even despair.

Controlling your emotions, learning how to heal after narcissistic abuse, and grounding are more than important for empaths—they are *crucial*.

What else is there to do?

Here are some additional strategies empaths can use to cope with the side effects of their typology:

- Laughing. You may have heard this before, but laughter really is the best medicine. When we laugh, our bodies and our spirits heal. Endorphins are released in the body, which helps not only our mood, but also our abilities to manage pain and anxiety levels. Laugh often to shed negative energies and recharge with positivity. Laugh with friends and family, laugh at TV series and movies, laugh with a good book in your hands. Laugh as much as you can.

- Essential Oils. Depending on how sensitive you are to scents, essential oils might prove to be a good ally against depression and anxiety. For instance, lavender oil is known to help with relaxation. There are also oils you can use for grounding, emotional protection, and every other need you might have as an empath. Furthermore, there are many ways you can use these oils. Everyone is different, so give essential oils a try and test out different options.

- Colors. There's a very good reason painting is therapeutic for empaths (and everyone else, really). Aside from the fact that painting and coloring are artistic activities that relax our brains and allow us to detach from the pain of the external world, they also work with one of the most powerful tools ever: color. Chromatic therapy can help empaths find their inner balance. So, use colors in your environment, play with them when painting and coloring, and dress in those colors that make you feel good. It might sound crazy, but all studies point to the fact that color therapy can *actually* work, so it is more than worth giving it a try (Azeemi & Raza, 2005).

- Shielding Visualization. This technique involves creating a mental shield of white or pink light around your body and extending it a few inches away from it. You should do this whenever you feel overwhelmed by your surroundings, such as when you are in a crowded mall or when you are attending a party with many guests. Take a few deep breaths and call on your "shield." It will help you protect yourself and feel better about the situation in which you find yourself.

- Clearly Defining Your Needs. This is not a technique per se, but a tip of advice all empaths should take and use, in my opinion. People find it difficult to relate to or interact with empaths precisely because they are so sensitive, but if you set your expectations and needs and clearly express them to people, they will know what to do and how to act around you. Believe it or not, the vast majority of people actually want to help you, but they don't know why. So being explicit about your expectations can be useful both on your end and on theirs.

- Spirit Animals. Like emotional shields, spirit animals can act to protect you. The key is finding that animal that suits you and your personality and making sure it's an animal you would trust to protect you. Whenever you feel overwhelmed, you can call on your spirit animal to help you out and protect you from the toxicity of the world around you.

Being an empath is not easy, but it doesn't have to prevent you from living your life in a beautiful and harmonious way. I trust that the tips and techniques presented so far will help you find a core of balance within yourself, so that you can achieve all the great things you set your mind to.

Remember: you are unique and amazing. Celebrate your empathy, but never allow the external world to wear you down. The right mindset will help you succeed at whatever you aim for!

Chapter 11: Supporting a Loved One Who Is an Empath

Clearly, being an empath can be quite the challenge, but sometimes, being around someone who is an empath can feel challenging as well. The main issues arise when empaths cannot communicate what they truly need from their loved ones and, in turn, their loved ones don't know how to behave around them.

What an empath is looking for, more than anything, is *support*. If you love an empath, you must be there for them and catch them when they fall, lift them up when they need it, and kindly remind them that they need to control their empathy for their own good.

To support a loved one who is an empath, you should keep in mind the following:

- Don't expect them to change, and never even try to require them to do it. Empaths are amazing human beings and we should celebrate them more often. What empaths need to do is not *change*, but calibrate their negative tendencies of accumulating everyone else's emotions.
- Don't cage them. An empath in a cage will wear down, and they will do it quickly. Allow your empath loved one to flow freely in the world at their own pace, by their own rules. They need space more than anything, precisely because they can so easily absorb external energies.
- Let them be alone. They need their alone time just as every human being needs air. Just because they want to retreat and be with themselves doesn't mean they don't love you. It just means they need to recharge for a little.
- Always trust what they say. Empaths are extremely hurt when you don't trust them or when you take them for fools. Trust what they say; what they are experiencing is not make-believe. Even more, trust them when they have a "gut feeling." Their intuition is truly one of their superpowers.

- Always be honest. Never lie to an empath. The moment you do this is the moment you have shattered their hearts into a million pieces—and that heart might never beat for you the same.
- Their love of animals is not a direct competition with their love of you. They really do love animals and plants, but that does not mean they do not love you too. Just as they need time alone, they need time with their wordless friends. Give this to them and they will be eternally grateful.
- Make them laugh. Empaths absorb a lot of toxicity, so making them laugh will help them shed the bad vibes and refill their hearts with positivity. The moment you make an empath laugh, you have literally lit up the room with their amazing energies.
- Understand that, for an empath, every emotion is experienced as if "on steroids." They cry harder, they laugh soundly, they are touched by the smallest things, and they can very easily shift their mood. For an empath, every single feeling is experienced at its maximum power. Don't be upset with them if they "overreact." They are, indeed, very sensitive.
- Don't be insecure around them. If you have insecurities (related to your relationship or anything else), try not to put these insecurities on your empath loved one. They need reassurance and support; anything insecure can easily send them spiraling down into a pool of negativity.
- Always be supportive. You might not always completely "get" your empath loved one, but even so, support them. At times, what they experience might seem odd to you. Support them anyway, and be by their side. They will be more than grateful.

Being around an empath can be a gift, but like most great things in life, it comes with a price. In this case, the price you have to pay is being the sturdy pillar upon which your empath loved one can lean when they need. It's not a huge price and, in time, you will definitely learn to love it—precisely because all the love and tenderness an empath can offer will win your heart.

Hey, it's Terry Lindberg,

Firstly thanks for completing my book this should set you up for success by putting you on the right path.

Remember, there are particular tools that you need not just to make your self-improvement journey easier, but make it more effective.

The first crucial tool you will need to make sure you have, so you do not fail, is the Ultimate Mindset Course by Intelligence Mastery.

As when starting your journey of self-improvement, the one thing that anybody who reaches success has; is a detailed plan in place.

To create a detailed plan to have a mindset shift that you'll need to set you up for success; you have to do endless amounts of research to get mental clarity, acquire new daily habits, and much more.

Sounds like hard work, right?

Well yes, it would be, but luckily for you, I have partnered up with Intelligence Mastery. Who are giving away their highly rated course that will give you all of the step-by-step process for shifting your mindset into gear seamlessly!

Best thing about this exclusive offer is it 100% FREE, no-strings-attached. Intelligence Mastery usually charge $297 for this exact same course to their customers

Make sure to search in on your browsers URL – free.intelligencemastery.com

Good luck on your journey and enjoy the course!

free.intelligencemastery.com

Conclusion

Being an empath is definitely not easy. But instead of looking at your typology as a chore, I urge you to do something else: embrace yourself.

You are one of the most unique flowers in the garden of Earth. You are good and kind, and you can make the world a better place with your love of everything and everyone. You are the definition of warmth and care. Within you lies the power of healing that the world needs so much these days.

What you need to do is fortify yourself against the negative influences and work on releasing your positivity out into the world. You don't have to give up on being who you are, you just have to learn how to calibrate those parts of you that are not doing you a service.

Can it be done?

Absolutely.

This book has shown you some of the essential techniques all empaths should master to protect themselves from bad energies and emotions and to win against their tendencies to absorb *everything* around them. From embracing your true self and knowing how your empathy affects your life to controlling your emotions and knowing how to find your center of balance, this book has covered the crucial ideas you need to keep in mind to live a happy life.

Yes, the world out there might be painful. As long as you know how to protect yourself from it, you can win at whatever you set your mind to, though. You are a superhero, one made of flesh and bones and capable of embracing the beauty of the world and multiplying it by a billion.

Love yourself, love the world, and stay safe!

If you enjoyed this book in anyway, an honest review is always appreciated!

CPSIA information can be obtained
at www.ICGtesting.com
Printed in the USA
BVHW051937080321
602010BV00012BA/1037